Like to
the Lark

Stuart Barnes

Stuart Barnes was born and grew up in Tasmania, educated at Monash University, Victoria, and now lives in Queensland, Australia. His first book, *Glasshouses* (University of Queensland Press, 2016), won the 2015 Arts Queensland Thomas Shapcott Poetry Prize, was commended for the 2016 FAW Anne Elder Award and shortlisted for the 2017 ASAL Mary Gilmore Award. Stuart's poetry has been widely anthologised and published, including in *The Anthology of Australian Prose Poetry*, *Best of Australian Poems 2022* and *POETRY* (Chicago), been nominated for the Pushcart Prize and been shortlisted for the Montreal International Poetry Prize, the Australian Catholic University Prize for Poetry and the Newcastle Poetry Prize. His 'Sestina after B. Carlisle' won the 2021/22 Gwen Harwood Poetry Prize. *Like to the Lark* is his second book.

Endorsements for *Like to the Lark*

Stuart Barnes holds space with words. With intimate knowing and acute sensitivity, he mindfully casts fragments of intense pleasure and pain to manifest beautiful lives beyond survival, recovery and healing, through a stunning array of poetic forms.

Like to the Lark fashions a tender, playful and wrenching relationality through nostalgia, trauma and beauty, so that we too can cry with black cockatoos at *the world's unrest* and sing with the moon, wind and trees, and that first light rising with the break of day.

NATALIE HARKIN

Stuart Barnes' poetry forges a unique path, expertly threading its way along the dividing line between vulnerability and rage, beauty and ugliness, the natural world and the synthetic, the old and the new, the sacred and profane, form and chaos. Risk-taking, moving, funny—always surprising—Barnes' poetry will remind you what it is to be alive.

MARIA TAKOLANDER

I don't think I've read a more joyful collection by a contemporary poet in a very long time. *Like to the Lark* is suffused with the joys of the world, or with the joys of a subject's relationship with the world. The book is also about the joys of verse-making: who else, but Stuart Barnes, would so effortlessly rhyme 'Macbeth' with 'bitter meth', or have so much fun writing such difficult forms as the sestina, the ghazal, or the sonnet? Reader, be prepared to have an experience that one does not often associate with contemporary poetry: prepare to enjoy yourself!

ALI ALIZADEH

Under the queer mirror ball of the moon and sunlight's blazing scalpel, Stuart Barnes shows us a degraded world that looks 'like death warmed up' while asserting that love will always be the 'vivider figure'. But doubt is never far away, as the poet asks how poems of love can exist in a context of homophobia, sexual violence and cultural amnesia around AIDS. The cry of the smalltown boy rises, but in brilliant counterpoint with the mature poet, whose technical bravura, intertextual wit and long view inform this incandescent, moving collection.

A. FRANCES JOHNSON

Alive with bravura queer energies, constrained loquacity and formal ambition, Stuart Barnes' *Like to the Lark* is a vibrant study in sophisticated provincialism. At once restless and arresting, urgent and laconic, Barnes playfully mines the resources of set form, refrain and repetition in this skilful, original and affecting lyric collection.

KATE LILLEY

Rich with puns, rhyme and assonance, roving from ghazal to acrostic to prose poem, and with references ranging from Greek myth to Auden and Kate Bush, Stuart Barnes' *Like to the Lark* queers language while freewheeling gloriously between traditions. But more than a masterclass in wordplay and citation, this collection offers a poignant, often explicit portrait of growing up and discovering sexuality in a sometimes brutal world where 'five men nearly broke me like a wishbone'. Moving between wit and grievance in the wake of trauma, Barnes, like the moon he so often cites, is a virtuosic 'Sinker of cliché / in cumulous seas'.

ANTHONY LYNCH

Stuart Barnes

Like to the Lark

UPSWELL

First published in Australia in 2023
by Upswell Publishing
Perth, Western Australia
upswellpublishing.com

This book is copyright. Apart from any fair dealing for the purpose of private study, research, criticism or review, as permitted under the *Copyright Act 1968*, no part may be reproduced by any process without written permission. Enquiries should be made to the publisher.

Copyright © 2023 by Stuart Barnes

The moral right of the author has been asserted.

ISBN: 978-0-6455369-8-0

 A catalogue record for this book is available from the National Library of Australia

Cover design by Chil3, Fremantle
Typeset in Foundry Origin by Lasertype

Upswell Publishing is assisted by the State of Western Australia through its funding program for arts and culture.

i.m. Noel Backhouse

but the sea

does not change

E. E. Cummings, '[as is the sea marvelous]'

•

i.m. Alexander 'Sandy' Mitchell

Recitar!... Vesti la giubba

Ruggero Leoncavallo, *Pagliacci*

I'm writing this for you, wherever you are, whoever is staring into your blue eyes.

David Malouf, 'Revolving Days'

•

What a lark! What a plunge!

Virginia Woolf, *Mrs Dalloway*

Contents

Off-world Ghazal   15

SOON THE MOON WILL SING
Persian Love Cake   19
Central Queensland Rondelets   20
Dust Bunnies   22
Sketching Aids   23
Abecedarian on Tension   24
How To Be a Good Gay in a Small Town   25
Duplex   26
The earth   27
Double Acrostic   29
Curtal Sonnet   30
Dinner with S. M. at Tandoori Den   31
The Pardoner   32
A–Z–A   34
Binary Tree Poem   35
In Heaven I'll be quite normal (or, Pentina to Doone Kennedy, after The Smiths)   36
Killing Bill or Whatever the Hell His Name Is (Battle Without Honor or Humanity)   37
Duplex   39
Ghazal: Tina   40
Sestina after B. Carlisle   41
Moon Speaks during Pasur   43

The Being	44
in the dark (wish)	45
Royal Poinciana (*Delonix regia*)	47
Duplex	48

WIND SINGS

Sestina: Rape	51
Bop: Apollo and Hyacinthos	53
Sex & Drugs & Goth Rock & Synth-pop & Hip-hop & New Wave & Funk/Soul Ghazal	54
Abecedarian on Provincial Drinking	55
#8WordStory	56
Rockhampton	57
GRINDR	59
Duplex	60
Spenserian Sonnet	61
bliss bliss (heart's beat)	62
Hamlet Without the Prince	67
Triolet on Receiving Email from C	68
Sestina: Pain	69
The Burnt-out Bougainvillea	71
Migraine	73
Petrarchan Sonnet	74
Tritina after The Cure	75
The 52-hertz Whale	76
Duplex	77
Sestina: Love	78

A TREE SINGS

Agave americana	83
Hills Hoist	84

In the navy	85
Moby-Dick; or, The Whale	86
I really hope you're doing okay	87
#8WordStory	88
Cerberus Watches Eros	89
At Seven Mile Beach	90
Duplex	91
Little Gilt	92
The morning fog	93
Luna, *Taxus baccata*	94
Sonnet 29	96
Duplex	97
Old Habits Die Hard	98
From the Morning	99
Happiness	102
You're	104
A Night Like This	105
Daphne's Tritina	106
Pentina after The Beatles	107
Moon's Étude	108
Immortal Jellyfish	109
Duplex	110
Boys Don't Cry	111
Coffee Grounds	112
Transcontinental Truth Ghazal	113
Notes on Form	115
References	119
Notes	121
Acknowledgements	127

Off-world Ghazal

> *I could hear*
> *the wild black cockatoos, tossed on the crest*
> *of their high trees, crying the world's unrest.*
> Judith Wright, 'Black Cockatoos'

Are you ready for the round-up, World?
Put your atlas down and feet up, World.

Give me the keys, the GPS. You
thrashed the hell out of the pickup, World.

What's your pleasure? Horse's Neck, Monkey
Gland, Cobra's Fang? The night's a pup, World.

Once you were razor-sharp, a Global
knife. Like stainless steel nerve cracks up, World.

Riled black cockatoos cried your unrest
(more than a storm in a teacup, World).

You unsealed records of days and nights
when earth's giant oak was wrought-up, World.

Into fantastic garlands of white
-leaved willow you wove buttercup, World.

You provoked Arctic ice, synthetic
ice, ICE. Your pick never let up, World.

Your coal mind and mechanical eyes
turned the sea of light downside up, World.

Glued to a screen you approved line
-ages', languages', lands' smash-up, World.

Don't move a muscle. Let me freshen
your drink. You look like death warmed up, World.

You built tall walls with stone-boat-loaded
stars thrown from an arc interrup— [World]

You guzzled every *radif* but one.
Your *takhallus* you covered up, World.

Peter Panesque you gurgled, thought your
-self clever, and never grew up, World.

Thunder, lightning didn't meet again.
In smoke your ambition went up, World.

Umpteen charges valuable as
Mar-a-Lago. Each is trumped-up, World?

A defamation suit? Colourful,
flimsy. In court it won't stand up, World.

No more tricks and abracadabra.
Your fascination is used up, World.

You wish to go the way of all flesh
imperially? A death cup, World.

You won't feel a thing. So long. Farewell.
Arrivederci. Bottoms up, World.

SOON THE MOON WILL SING

Persian Love Cake

My purple-shirted prince is
waking in the Queensland sun
Today's his birthday
I sliver green pistachios

Baking in the Queensland sun
I twirl dried rosebuds
sliver green pistachios
swirl golden bulbs in a pan

I twirl dried rosebuds
pulse black aphrodisiacs
swirl golden bulbs in a pan
lick stars of almond praline

the impulse paradisiac
He is rosewater cream
starry, like almond praline
and cool as lemon icing

He is rosewater cream
a purple-shirted prince, is
cooling, like lemon. I sing
Today's his birthday!

Central Queensland Rondelets

Anemones
scrutinise the Keppels—fish tanks'
anemones
colourless as frangipanis
rattling wooden spoons against shanks.
No moon. A dullish hoodlum yanks
anemones.

•

Black fruit bats drop
mangoes on starred corrugations.
Black fruit bats' drop
-pings strip Polaris paint. A crop
of tower lights' exclamations
incites sour abbreviations
—black fruit bats drop.

•

Curlews, terror
-ised, squeeze egg-embellished earth, freeze.
Curlews, terror
-ised, widen wings, hiss, dance error
-less dances. Ballerina-ease
fascinates vertebrates that tease
curlews' terror.

•

Dugong dugon
snuffs seagrass through a shiny trike.
Dugong dugon
survives props—a fluke. Woebegone
subtropical waters.   ~~~   A bike
of scientists sculptures lifelike
Dugong dugon.

•

Estuarine crocs
—dozens of Napoleonic
estuarine crocs
—bite the bullet, fight—aftershocks.
(What beat the brain of Chthonic
Man who beat in that iconic
estuarine croc's?)

Dust Bunnies

So small, so mousy. We seem powerless,
but we seize web of spider, hair of you.
We swallow pollen (but are flowerless)
and carrot atoms (these we curse). Please view
our Lilliputian lightning show. Wasp stings,
red bedbug beaks and cockroach claws are sung
as if by Shakespeare's sisters into strings
that in the night go bump (so hold your tongue!).
But we are more alive than dead. Here, see
the spores of mushrooms plume in us, dust mites
assemble prams and rams, and DDT
take stock, take stock. Micrometeorites,
our stomach stones, are sweet. We eat, we eat
and like a rocky planet we accrete.

Sketching Aids

On a queen
size sheet two
men, one dog

in between
their legs, blue
set squares. Fog

and Grief preen,
then rule who
will prologue

the blown spleen,
the skin's *Phew* ...
the cells' slog.

Abecedarian on Tension

> *the wrecked thing that could*
> *not bear the light nor hide*
> *hobbled in its own blood.*
>
> Gwen Harwood, 'Barn Owl'

Acceleration. First lesson. *Don't*
be nervous—your vocal cords'll
constrict even more. We might
duet. Grey sky-silhouetted, creased, taut.
Electrocuted like a criminal. Black
fruit bat (*Pteropus alecto*). Alecto—Fury.
Guilty!—power lines' night-verdict—no jury.
Humankind
—invertebrate—is fated to wreck things.
Just take Harwood's barn owl.
Knuckle-white, I grip the wheel.
Lurch of vehicle.
Machinegunfire from the hood.
Now it could be a faun's umbrella, inside
-outed in a snowstorm. Cloudburst. Im
-patiently I wait, hazards' orange
queering the bodgie bitumen.
RACQ's haggard feller
sneers about timing belts,
tensioners, pulleys. My
unease rises. Wolfish Agriopas'
viscera. One of Geryon's lost
wings. The mane of
Xanthos. A hearse strains, black and
yellow. I curse the mechanic who,
Zeus-smug, strung up the Subaru.

How To Be a Good Gay in a Small Town

for Leigh Backhouse

Install the one-star black-and-yellow app.
Gang up with John the Practised at Queens Park,
Park Avenue (don't be quick-witted). Snap
Orion's head off, snuff the new moon's spark.

Don't rant and rave (*The hunts of Kodiak!*)
while cramming gulping bulbs with bitter meth
or bumping K from tits in Zodiac;
don't spell out why John mustn't say Macbeth

inside the Pilbeam; swill your Beam and Cokes
with equal swag, get off on shots of *Butch!*,
high-five each other, whack the butt of jokes
(the fag who looks like Old You, squeaking *Putsch!*),

then stagger to the jagged light without
a glint of camp, a hint of standing out.

Duplex

Walking iris, Apostle plant (Neomarica gracilis)

Rhythm's afoot. My fingers step to earth.
They put down roots. They stamp and stamp their whorls.

    Worms lay down routes—a red stampede—air whirls.
    The sun, another plantigrade, treads heat.

The sun, another plantigrade, spreads heat
—I raise a dozen incandescent masks.

    Abuzz, I lower incandescent masks,
    I blow faces, ephemeral but famed

bright-blue faces. Perennial and famed,
my fingertips tingle with certainty.

    My fingertips tingle with certainty
    —I turn and turn twelve diminutive selves.

I turn and turn twelve diminutive selves.
Rhythm's afoot. My fingers step to earth.

The earth

turns to the moon as if
it were the one and only
satellite capable, tonight,
of attending to grievances we
heave at the could
-have-been in our sleep.

The moon used to sleep
with one eye open, mail coif
riveted to a skull that would
annihilate horror with only
a nod, riveted by the we
-stern winds of day and night,

all eyes riveted on it. Tonight
(and every other) the moon's asleep
at the wheel. Fearful, we
give it an earful of sans serif
Riveting? You've a face only
pareidolia could

love! A lone rust-red cloud
-tail's deformed by night's
hammers like a rivet. The moon only
has eyes for itself, it needs no beauty sleep
now. It's absorbed too much kif,
performed away from its krewe.

We call for it to overawe
us like creamy amber cloud
-berries. If only we could be sportif,
the moon our tennis ball tonight.
If only tonight we could sleep,
the moon overlooking us as only

celestial bodies can. It's only
a question of time before we,
chillingly extravagant, sleep
still as Illinois' mastodons. *Would
you like blood, moon?* Tonight
(and every other) it cold-shoulders this apéritif.

*Only you can slow us, sleep
-ing policeman in the night sky!* We
harden, no-good riveters, under the dark leitmotif.

Double Acrostic

Did he who made the Lamb make thee?
William Blake, 'The Tyger'

Horror, in the beginning. Folding, unfolding of
universal holes—when, where, why. *Apologies*, I
murmured, kissing the salty feet of hypnagogic
apparitions. Vanity fathered nightmares—anti
-neoplastics, the purple people eaten alive,
I am Nemo. A sea reddened by execution,
Marram grass rhizomes tuned in the dunes, an ascetic
moulded from mercury. Photosensitivity
underlaid bone. '¡*Ándale! ¡Arriba!*'—a TV
near childhood. To ride the white horse of black death (XIII),
or riot, Ed? Am I truly a happy number?
Did they who made humanity make me? Amanu
-ensis, they're igniting subjection—baby-blue pills!

Curtal Sonnet

With a nod to Gerard Manley Hopkins

ENTRIP does not contain any safe benefits.
    It is not approved for use in hives of aggro child
        -ren. Yellow tongue, nose-bruising, swelling of the eyes
are highly likely, the usual seizures, fevers, fits.
      A tall glass of Parkinson's, a psychiatrist's overactive mouth
        are mild
          -er. Forget blue, yellow, brown—one size

fits all. Feeling violent, heartless? Grip
    pharmacists' hallucinations, swallow doctors' chests. Wild
      -'s the divided dose times three. How else can we
        characterise
unhealing. EN(DANGER THIS)TRIP? EN(DANGER THIS)TRIP?
        Reflux the highs.

Dinner with S. M. at Tandoori Den

The city
fumes. Cabs cold
-shoulder me.

Train's pity.
Perfumed, kohled
men, herb tea.

Still pretty.
Wink. Frames' gold
flames as he,

still witty,
still controlled,
speaks of sea

gods, gritty
eyes, patrolled
kidneys. We

sit. Spitty
weathers hold
off. *You see,*

I'm Mitty
-esque, an old
shell.   I see

Aditi.
Marigold.
Smell sweet ghee.

The Pardoner

*With thanks to Dustin Brookshire,
author of* To the One Who Raped Me

On the wall a small plate
of sunshine shifted position
bit by bit. He'd've had me pick from Gothic headstones.
While he washed I turned the deco doorknob with
military precision. Briefs, wallet, keys.

Though on ice, *To the One Who Raped
Me* is prostrate with hope. My own mind
is my own church. In the sack
I'm no longer an African cat.
Night terrors give way to dreams.

The fever's gone
(Zelitrex a zeppelin
floating at low altitude),
the long weekends (smashed
on Yellow Birds,

Horse's Necks, Elephant Gimlets,
the vapours of
fags/cowboy killers/cigarettes,
scored by Tina's grey-jewelled paws
—enough

to crystallise hair).
I've eaten
my fill of sleazy smiles,
colour
handkerchiefs rippling

denim pockets, matchsticks
thrilling skin. Entirely
guilty of subversion
I've murmured *He loves me, he
loves me lots*, quilting **GRINDR**'s fakery.

I've dreamed of amnesia.
I've dreamed of Major Nelson. Here,
I've dreamed of seven hours' revenge, criminal
of zero variety
—a kelson of the creation hooked

into him, into him, into him.
Such sweet thunder
—Amazonian queen, I ration
Brookshire's chapbook. Away
with the houselights. Douse impossibility.

Candles laugh in the face of the dark.
Post-burial, what'll I eat,
will I starve. The wattle spills globose light
over Ariel—Ariel, Ariel, Ari, he
who drugged and raped and pardoned me.

A–Z–A

arsenic (n.), late 14c., "yellow arsenic, arsenic trisulphide," from Old French *arsenic*, from late Greek *arsenikon* "arsenic", from Old Iranian **zarna-* "golden," like Flores Žuta Osa's slivovitz. A man swung time with Ginger Rogers in New York City—his original name was Frederick Austerlitz. *Also Sprach Zarathustra*'s first stereophonic recording was made by Reiner, Fritz. Agee, Leon fashioned one of the world's largest gems—the American Golden Topaz. At high school my *Assez* enlaced my *Asseyez*. A double abecedarian's opening line anchors *A* and launches *Z*. Zaryab's parents zinged from Iran to Australia the year the King swinged, for the last time, each coxa. *Zarb*-brilliance fills their villa. Zaryab's fingers' upstrokes are thrilling—so too the way he plays Frank Zappa's 'The Legend Of The Golden Arches' on the *zampoña*. Zhang Yimou's first *wuxia*'s my favourite picture; Zaryab's is *Arsenic and Old Lace*, directed by Frank Capra. Zaryab and I morning-float among *Zostera tasmanica*; after noon we spoon on *Zoysia japonica*. Zaryab whispers, as we drift off, *I wonder if Zambia's clouds still nicker at the dazzling stripes of Crawshay's zebra* ...

Binary Tree Poem

Monthly, the moon's a full-blown wad of chewing gum,
juicy fruit amid wriggly leaves. Monthly, the moon's
a full-blown wad of chewing gum (sodiumless, unlike the moon).

Monthly, the moon's juicy fruit amid wriggly leaves,
longer-lasting. Seas are hauled ashore monthly, the moon's
juicy fruit amid wriggly leaves, fingerless, limbless, trunkless.

A full-blown wad of chewing gum (sodiumless, unlike the moon,
the fascinating artificial moon), a full-blown wad of chewing gum
(sodiumless, unlike the moon) is flavored by Mars, Incorporated.

Longer-lasting seas are hauled ashore, fingerless, limbless, trunkless.
The fascinating artificial moon is flavored by Mars, Incorporated.

In Heaven I'll be quite normal
(or, Pentina to Doone Kennedy, after The Smiths)

but in Tasmania I'm
diabolical, quite
the opposite of normal
—*Faggot! Poof! Grim Reaper!* (barbarism begins at home)—I thank
the other kids with gory smiles. *Goodness* ...

sighs my mother, bleaching and starching shirts. *Goodness* ...
sighs the chaplain, tamping Psalms into my throat until I'm
gulping, gaga. *Thank*
you for opening up, though there's quite ...
sighs the headmaster ritually, *a ways to go before* ... Normal

-'s how I'll feel seven years on, sculpting 'Mis-Shapes'. *Normal*,
seventeen years on, -'ll compact my foundation. Goodness,
even The Monster Ball Tour in twenty-one'll leave me quite
breathless. Heaven knows I'm miserable now, I'm
low as all hell. So who to thank

for this weakness at the knees for Jesus? Thank
you, vicar in a tutu, for passing out behind the altar (a normal
Sunday morning—all-night spritzers at La Cage)—I'm
renewing the vow (*No goodness*
in homo adulthood). Quite

horrifying—in '58, Noel shot himself, his Bert got three years. Quite
terrifying—I might get up to twenty-one. So who to thank
for this panic? No truth, beauty or goodness
at the dead centre of Lorna Doone 'Quite Normal'
Pleasance Kennedy. In seven years I'm

going to cruise the strait, a handsome devil. I'm not quite super
-normal so I'll manage my pleasance, thank the Lord for His goodness.

Killing Bill or Whatever the Hell His Name Is (Battle Without Honor or Humanity)

No one expected the second coming
out

—a burst rubber, a premature
BOOM!

PEP, you echoed. *I'll drive you to the local clinic*

first thing in the morning.

His speechlessness a stun
grenade,

ignored calls
blast

mines. Minutes
later,

GRINDR's miss
-iles.

    •

Small—the Beef Capital—the bit of
linoleum

on which Bill or whatever the
hell

his name is
fixes

a gaze blank and
pitiless

as the sun in
Coles'

old-fashioned produce
section.

Your imagined visor blazes
blackly,

like the Bride's, your Kawasaki sets off
yellowly.

Duplex

Eremophila 'Blue Horizon'

I've always adored the deft desert,
its transformative blues and solitude.

> I transform the bluesy solitude
> of winter—I polish small gold trumpets

—gold-tinted blue-tongues polish off my trumpets
—I raise my hands, lanceolate and blue.

> Lancelot was raised by hands of blue,
> I improvise—I play blue notes. *Roll low*

my soul cries. Playing blue notes, rolling low,
I weave the earth and the atmospheres.

> I grieve earth's people, flatten their fears,
> weather the emu, the stormy blues.

The emu untethers glorious blues.
I've always adored the deft desert.

Ghazal: Tina

All I ever wanted was to nuzzle Tina.
Within a month I needed to guzzle Tina.

Carpets' colours started speaking to me.
Jewish friends echoed *Tov mazel, Tina*.

At an all-boys enclosure I flunked chemistry,
but mastered $C_{10}H_{15}N_1$—your puzzle, Tina.

Your sweet puffs toyed with my libido—Poof!
—& crowned my scalp with monkey puzzle, Tina.

Your biker's coffee breath phosphorised my nose.
So I fashioned a shatterproof muzzle, Tina,

from the sizzling shards of a nuclear blast,
cooked shabu-shabu then this ghazal, Tina.

Sestina after B. Carlisle

My dying friend maintains Heaven
hallows only one queen: *Hell is
just around the corner, like a
gaudy shopping centre, a place
of no rest day nor night.* Hot on
my heels, the Devil's moving earth

and heaven to drag me from Earth
—say yes to drag!—to his heaven,
where KS-coloured light grows on
devilwood and angel dust is
pain's composer. Can't you feel Place
de la Concorde's wings shudder? A

Gabriel created it. A
wild Gabriel comes to me—Earth
doesn't know where to turn, I place
bets on Red. Do you want Heaven
or Las Vegas? he trumpets. Fizz
of feathers. Tell the tycoon on

high, I wave, to leave a light on
—and that I never wanted a
rich man. The syndrome my soul is
bedevilled by was sent to Earth
by the consuming fire of Heav'n.
Syndrome, *from Greek* syndromos, *place

where several roads meet.* God, my place
concatenates multitudes. John
Waters' Divine endorsed Heaven,
but my whitish tongue arrows a
Fuck you very much! to God. Earth
turns swords into ploughshares. Gee whiz,

I'm not good to go—hold my vis
-à-vis with the Valet de Place
—hold his runaway horses. Earth
—glorious! It'll go-go on.
Have I ever told you I'm A
-neg? God, blood enraptures Heaven.

On Vespas my dying friend is
a daredevil, gold as 'Heaven
Scent"s placets, summer rain, shared earth.

Moon Speaks during Pasur

You will never be over me
You bark at me, want me on a stick
a purifying fishermoon
playing with a full deck

You bark at me, want me on a stick
golden as a Kushan coin
Playing with a full deck
I think I hung myself and the stars

Golden as a Kushan coin
you ask for me, you ask for me
I think I hung myself and the stars
—don't cast beyond me

You ask for me, you ask for me
Stop mooning over your hand
don't cast beyond me
—I wield seven clubs

Stop mooning over your hand
A purifying fishermoon
I wield seven clubs
You will never be over me

The Being

*Representatives of the gay community
are no better than Saddam Hussein*

former Ulverstone, Tasmania councillor Jack Breheny

I am fallen, your arch-villain
(but I ought to be your Adam!)
and a million

other fish in the Chilean
sea. Two-backed, no better than Saddam
Hussein. The brassy Brazilian

Big Horse, the headless, reptilian
purist haunting London's Madame
Tussauds, Robert Mugabe's crocodilian

former right-hand man. Dylan
Thomas' shapeshifter, the macadam
-ised hooves of Sylvia Plath's stallion. Amoxicillin

for Zilzie Beach's stingrayed tourists. Bolivian
marching powder scouring septa. Adam
Ant's 'Phoenix' and 'Vampires'. A vanillin

-clawed migraine. Rising Maldivian
waters (*We, my dears, don't give a damn
the searing winds hiss*). This villan
-elle, elbowing towards oblivion.

in the dark (wish)

mobiles' torches, little red flying foxes' eyeshine   *I fin*
-ished digging myself out of that hole in spring   bass-pulse
we sat at the dance floor's outpost for a spell   minutes
flushed as if they'd inspired poppers
for the love of God, I laughed with Michael,
this is Newish Me—no dope, in high spirits   diva
-bloom   *always got my eye on you*   noses rubbed, he
bubbled the door   I bought a second
& final pint   *hello uh-huh no thanks goodbye*
to the tattooed, black-bearded bear   suddenly I was
twisted by disco   strobes unloosed the mirror ball
-'s I   good sense vanished like a wish
-ing well's ting   carpet gargled the Nikes shined
for Michele's wedding   i tried to stay one
jump ahead of him   dead asleep, my hairy legs   stabs
of piano   *rhythim is rhythim, strings*
of life, Mayday, swishing his hoodie's sleeves   i was belted
towards a neon arrow, stood in a Never Never
-ish torrent   in windows' reflections, sallowish skin   thin

-king, a blepharospastic eye, contracted   *uh-uh*
—thataway   aphonic, i melted among bodies unrivalled
as dayflies   for the love of short-sightedness
would i give my eyeteeth?   at teenagehood's edge
i also walked the plank   a second date   twenty-two years i
frothed at the mouth, crossing more states than the Missouri
don't ever miscalculate cold intuition's fury   hope
-clouds glimmered   blue skies, gold sun   today I danced
with Prudence   the one who's all eyes might turn
back time   i spied my voice, materialised
every which way   five men nearly broke me like a wish
-bone   beams issued from my thighs   *uh, fellers? don't*
think he's— stay (faraway, so close!)   latch's
snick   mobiles' torches, crocodilian eyeshine   i came

to myself on the cubicle's mattress   disco doused me, a little
yellowish light   i spelled *dee   o   i   tee   jay   u
ess   tee*   hotel eiderdown swaddled me   should I unwish
this history, Ruth? *visualise neutrality*   night
-'s wings of desire swish as far as the eye can see

Royal Poinciana (*Delonix regia*)

And Sampson said, Let me die with the Philistines.
And he bowed himself with all his might
Judges 16:30

For too long I have lived with these barbarians. One dares to lumber around beneath me, the other mows and mows while mumbling *Shallow*. I am sick to death of wickedness, coarse skins and narrow minds, upside-down limbs. My breath is rooted in kindness, skin smooth and mind broad, my limbs shoot for the stars. One brute grumbled about my glorious crown and thrown shade, airy flamboyance and spilt beans, phoenix-tails embellishing the earth so the other unleashed its glittering silver tongue. This made me hot under the collar. This opened the door to the borer. It will not do, it will not do. Nothing, nothing will soothe my wounds. *Suburban, weedy, invasive*, these perennial prunes say, but I predate footpaths, brickwork, masonry. They nicked my little jacket, they tricked me into being, but I am sap of no thing, no thing now. Once, my immaculate limbs sang to them of love. Soon the moon will sing of Madagascar and I will wow each flower strewn and bow myself with all my might.

Duplex

Aloe 'Mighty Orange'

In winter I swing mighty orange bells
—honeycombers and honeyeaters glow.

      Honeycombers and honeyeaters glow
      —even my tapered green fingers flush.

Shapely green thumbs uneven earth. This flush
of youth is as truthful as Latin.

      Love, too, is as truthful as Latin,
      which can be tough and can be tender.

I can be tough, and I can be tender
—frost can knock me over with a feather.

      Frost can knock me over with a feather,
      but I'm immune to Roundup's amber plumes.

Immune to Roundup's climbing amber plumes
in winter, I swing mighty orange bells.

WIND SINGS

Sestina: Rape

i.m. Anita Cobby

When I was a kid it hid in our red crêpe
paper crowns, the scrape
of fair knees, my mother's grape
hyacinths. At eight I watched it fly from behind a drape,
the abduction, gang-rape
and murder of Anita Cobby. Nirvana's 'Rape

Me', Tori Amos' 'Me And A Gun'—white grape
-fruit. I was eighteen when DATE-RAPE
donged. *No such thing as male rape*
flared. No rape report, no rape
kit. When I split the pith of this rape
three sweethearts laughed in my face. Rape

bird-dogged me—the grapevine, the sky-scrape
-red air; crepe myrtle, broomrape;
crêpes Suzette, red grape
-fruit. I squirmed at university—Zeus' rape
of Leda, her nape caught in his bill; trape
-zius myalgia fanning out; the scrape

of pear trees. Rape
-enclosure, my fourth sweetheart. Hard rape
counselling. I forced down *Law & Order: SVU*—rape
-exposure after rape
-exposure—finally, I stopped the keen. Rape
-opiates? All stepped down. I cared for myself with rape

(*Brassica napus*). I devoured rape.
I cleaned my teeth with the bones of rape.
I was forty when GANG-RAPE
gonged. I was mellow as rape
vinegar. I pared terror like grape
-fruit. Two beloveds denied my rape

-song. Seven repaired my red trape
-ze. It opened me like a window, this rape.
Here, see its material drape:

```
r           a p             e
r         a    p            e
r       a        p          e
r     a            p        e
r   a                p      e
r a                    p    e
r   a                  p    e
r     a              p      e
r       a          p        e
```

Rape declared nuclear war, but I am not rape
-torn or -weary, a rape trophy or poet. Rape,
I've got my eye on you. Rape, prepare. ~~Rape.~~

Bop: Apollo and Hyacinthos

I have AIDS. The Touchfone's crimson Recall
button gushed *He showed you thumbs and fingers are
all, a man can adore the abnormal heart
-beat of another, Cyndi Lauper's third sin
-gle's true colours* (introducing it in
Paris in the '80s she said, head aflame

A bop a day keeps the doctor away!)

I'm finished. Decades later his Renaissance
fingers feathered oars, short stories and mine
as limned in gold we immortalised time
after time over artichokes and wine.
But revelation's summer and autumn scram
-bled light, precipitating winter. Triple
-tailed, like his HAART, the comet vamped. High on God
-knows-what, I arrowed onto the roof. *A Hale,*

a Bopp a day keeps the doctor away!

Morphine's woolly fingers pulled on Remembrance
Day. One cool morning he left his engine
running—'Boy, What A Night'—while I shot a road
-side poppy farm's warning. Did I dream I drove
all night, pursuing spring, uprooting each 'Blue
Jacket', face aquiver? Who let in the rain?

A bop a day keeps the doctor away.

Sex & Drugs & Goth Rock & Synth-pop & Hip-hop & New Wave & Funk/Soul Ghazal

Not even *it* could titillate a stiff, e-adult
-.com. We'll be there in a jiffy! Insult

Charlie, Lucy, Molly, Roxy & Tina at your
own risk until we reach the cliffy, tumult

-uous heroine = you owe us heroin.
Vault them if you can, the squiffy, vult

-urous blockheads. The Goths were mocked,
but goth is an excessively sniffy subcult

-ure. Take Ultravox's Midge Ure
with a grain of salt. Divvy 'A Salt

With A Deadly Pepa'.
Got everything? Spliff, E, Cult

-ure Club's *Kissing To Be Clever*
(third single turned a spiffy somersault

up the charts, slave only to 'Billie Jean')?
Rave about this ghazal's iffy penult

-imate stanza. Rockhamptonites mutter
Sup, mate   I'm amped out   Shiv multicult—

Abecedarian on Provincial Drinking

*AIDS
bomb!* boomed the FIFOers. *Git yer AIDS away from our mate, ya
    filthy fag!*
catapulting me into that '95 midnight—high school's star footballer,
dolled up in Johnnie Walker Blue and opportunity, pushing
everyone
—fawners, bartenders, busboys—to chorus, over silty jazz,
Gays give the gift of AIDS!
Had a rep to maintain, my friend pouring European beer, I suppose.
    Later,
in noisy lino corridors, he'd crimson, lower eyes. Dumb blond
jock, on the other hand, blitz
-krieged until end-of-year phys. ed.—one rugby ball, two
    legs interlacing, as
luck would have it, three fractures in his talus (and poise, poor dear).
    At the hands of those
miners packing XXXX Bitter and immunity in the pub on Friday
night I would've been a mass
of cliff-foot fragments had I
put a foot wrong. Sweet Jesus, I held up my hands
—quietness swarmed like a maculopapular
rash. *Never wrestle with
swine*, my grandfather, supping home-brew from a
toby jug, once cautioned. Though no lager lashed my back, though
unlit streets leashed their
vehemence as I scrambled home, bush stone-curlews, those nocturnal
    augurs,
wept *Teenage experience will
Xerox itself again*. I still get night sweats
—yobbos and yuppies, tanked on swill and top-shelf grog, drilling the
    earth and milling about like
zombies.

#8WordStory

Happiness is black cockatoos squabbling in the eucalypts.

Rockhampton

The
City
of
Sin,
Sweat,
Sorrow

(Sorrow).
The
Sweat
City.
Sin?
O f—!

O f—!
—Sorrow
-'s in
the
City
-'s wet!

Sweat
of
City,
sorrow.
The
sin

-'s in
sweat
—teehee!
O f—!
—Sorrow
City …

City
-'s *in!*
Sorrow
-'s wet.
O f—
the ...

the City
of Sin,
Sweat, Sorrow!

GRINDR

Modern-day ENTERPRISE TINNED MEAT CHOPPER (a cast-iron antique, dignified though its retainer squeals SCREW THIS RING UP TIGHT). Does my black-and-yellow mask appeal, the illusion of absolute freedom? Edit Profile > Body Type > Do Not Show/ Toned/Average/Large/Muscular/Slim/Stocky (the prime cuts two and five). Are you marbled? Expect to be parboiled. Are you dark meat? Dredging is forecast. Are you white meat and lean? You'll feed multitudes! Stuff the forefinger. Knuckle down. Linger over a profile, the illusion of a cube, nose the illusion of Wagyu. Ham it up with the jerky, the meatball, the boar. So many bears in so many squares! One week Peter, one week Pierre. One a rack, the other a rack. Isn't this voicelessness bliss, this mincing air! Terms of Service: I am the only means of grazing in this Capital of Beef. My addictive crystals sauté whorls, yet leave no visible trace (I am never subcutaneous, intravenous, intramuscular). I twang your hock, I butterfly, I slice against your grain. I French extremities, I split your wishbone. I never cater love, you chump. Settings > Privacy > Delete Profile > Are you sure you want to delete—

Duplex

'HIV Used to Be a Death Sentence.'
TIME's certainty angers my +ve friend.

    Time's uncertainty soothes my +ve friend
    whose watch chirps hourly from its black box.

We watch superb parrots crowd black box
hollows, YouTube Loleatta H., Black Box.

    No feeding tube, no Tasmanian blackwood box.
    My friend's adamant. *I want to ride on time.*

My friend's adamantine clock keeps good time.
He dyes his hair international orange.

    I dye my hair international orange
    to correspond to aeroplane's black boxes.

I correspond with honey bees' white boxes.
It used to be A-plus as hives', death's sentience.

Spenserian Sonnet

SUMATRAN will understand your aura.
It is not controlling like a pharmacist.
It is not cold or bitter like a doctor.
It is pink as the concern of an agonist.

One dose and you will smoke relief. Persist
-ent purple ears, sore jaw? Two-pack
of lies. You will not flush, tremor, fit, faint or blist
-er. Forty-year-old male? No heart attack.

It is hearsay, that it is sick, the pack
-aging—stroke it. Don't be so sensitive,
Shorty—migraine will not come back.
This medicine is highly selective.

It does not contain gluten,
wort or sugar. Give it your full atten—

bliss bliss (heart's beat)

With a nod to Melvin Dixon

I meditate
salute the sun

jump rope for heart
one two three four

swim laps for lungs
five six sev'n eight

write poetry
good *kokoro*

zip my suitcase
ignore the hunch

each window's wide
'Bliss' (Live) is free

a Toll Mack truck
arrests my drive

stereo plunge
-dives into wreck

•

tossed cross of pain
on shoulders, neck

hot clot of shock
arrhythmic cop

*Take photos, move
your vehicle—*

*My ears are throb
-bing, vision's blurred—*

*You're blocking this
arterial—*

*My car's a squished
accordion—*

a vein pops, *Move
your vehicle—*

*The vertigo—
For fuck's sake, drive!*

•

in limbs & trunk
electric shocks

the hard neck brace
& spinal board

Emergency's
tranquillity

the Niked nurse
with cannula

the brilliance of
the fentanyl

the CT scan
I meditate

the lost report
soft-eyed, I wait

*Your brain is un
-remarkable*

•

disjointed sen
-tences & words

I hit the wall
I black out twice

the sirens call
BP's real high

Emergency's
disharmony

the spiky nurse
with cannula

the bruit of Doc
Automaton

*A pinched nerve or
a TIA*

*take aspirin
don't drive—one week*

•

I meditate
take aspirin

read poetry
aid memory

the MRI
I meditate

No TIA
don't drive—one week

more H_2O
no added salt

carotid du
-plex ultrasound

I can't dismiss
my blood's *bliss bliss*

Your arteries
are beautiful

•

I meditate
salute the sun

jump rope for heart
one two three four

swim laps for lungs
five six sev'n eight

write poetry
good *kokoro*

more H_2O
no added salt

desensitise
myself, I drive

my frigatebird
pumps up its pouch

*The triumph of
an upbeat heart!*

Hamlet Without the Prince

Vulnerable as forest red-tailed black cockatoos, you went south the day the stock market headed south. I consoled myself by re-watching *North by Northwest*, filmed partly on location in South Dakota and California, and inspiration for South by Southwest, which takes place in America's Lone Star State. *The Secret History*'s Charles Macaulay wound up washing dishes in a Texan diner, but was born in Virginia with a silver spoon in his mouth. Richard Papen returned to The Golden State and read the Jacobean dramatists. If I were a Greek god I'd be Notus. I am but mad north-north-west. When the wind is southerly I know a hawk from a handsaw. While at college Elizabeth Bishop wrote about a hawk, but I'm more enamoured of *North & South*'s laméd poem. My maternal grandmother, Betty, who lived and died in the small northern town where she was born, played bridge in a silver lamé dress, always South, always partnered with North. Elizabeth Bishop sailed south to Brazil, I flew north in Australia, to where the Banksian black cockatoo's *kree* can bring the air to a standstill. I used to be a sucker for a man with a mouth full of South, a tongue like a southern cassowary's claw, but the nickname Wombat, after the southern hairy-nosed species, is awful. It's easy to find true north if you stop playing 'A Forest' by The Cure.

Triolet on Receiving Email from C

My iMac's a new sort of medium.
I slip on C's slippers, debrief the moon,
intractable, slouchy as tedium.
My eye macks a new sort of medium,
grief pouches like *Selenipedium*
orchids' flowers. The awkwardest month's June.
My iMac's a new sort of medium.
I slip on C's slippers, debrief the moon ...

Sestina: Pain

Bloodied knees—my mother butterflied pain.
I wheezed like Walter from *Love and Pain
and the Whole Damn Thing* in winter. Pain
grew in my limbs nightly—I flew to Spain
in trances, entrancing as Peter Pan, pain
-lessness blooming like agapanthus. I pain

-stakingly staked out horses, my father pain
-fully pulleyed gorse. At eleven I baked *pain
au chocolat, pain au levain* and *petit pain*,
sold my soul to Betty Wright's 'No Pain,
No Gain' and Betty White's golden pain
relief. T-ball was frightening as pain

-tball, puberty fiery as Tybalt, a pain
in my neck, my gut, my butt. House of Pain
jumped me, jumped around, acid house spilled from Pain
Killers' decks, *I will come by you into Spain*
filled God's house, enlivening pane upon pane
—I saw another heaven. It was pain

-sworthy, unearthing Gwen Harwood's 'Pain
flows through to your brush-tip and there is changed'. Pain
dipped its toes in my backbone's waters, clacked *Pain!
Pain! Pain!*, a sort of *art autre*, southwards. *Pain
perdu* wasn't lost on your mouth. ~~Champagne~~
Sparkling white jonesed the ringing light of a pain

-ting by Louise Hearman. A world fear campaign
vowed **FALLEN ANGELS! DISEASE!**, but in Pain
Court, Ontario we whirled, snow angels. *Airpane
Jerry!* sang my nephew. *Not now—afterpain*,
shot my sister, hanging up. You offered *pain
doré*. Lurid tourists snapped Tommy the Pain

-ted Turtle. I hurtled *tres insultos* at Spain,
but even so loved wholly, like Walter. P.A.I.N.
—Nan Goldin's—was aureate, unlike other pain
(ἄλλος + ὀδύνη), emboldened by half-skull pain.
With stillness and a mirror my pa-in
-law forked and forked his phantom limb pain.

Pain kneaded your thin-flued heart—fingers, pain
-terish, blued. Hair Payne's grey, eyes blue as Paine
Towers—paintable, you. Now who'll share my *gros pain*?

The Burnt-out Bougainvillea

Some thing has taken the place

of the bougainvillea, something biblical. Teeth
have taken out vibrant lumps
like prehensile, opaque
starfish. Some thing has crazed the bark,

quelling its wear
-ability. *Blood will tell*
toll the fronds of a Cuban Royal under
which the man sporting a tanga tans. Tang of charcoal sports and falls.

If some thing can insinuate
itself between thorny green bones
then the stones
concealing black field crickets

(*They squeal*, you say, *like next door's babies or
coal train brakes*) will incinerate among
antique crackled bowls
and daytime's undertones run.

Alice Coltrane spun once,
in the barmy reefer spring
—'Isis and Osiris' did
its nut. No balm for the lip

of the nearby reef, each tapered flower galactic-white,
each bridge
of this paperflower one
hell of a black. Once a person

-age, the staggering tanned man whose cat-tails
droop and doll eyes bobble below a moon austere
as porcelain. Its water
hoards i

-dolise gravity. For the hearts' doorstep
this is neither here nor there.
You and I live in a glasshouse
—hordes of digs. Some thing at the dead centre of us

digs in heels. The bougainvillea heals, heals.

Migraine

A pain in the neck.
Brume spuming at your eye's dead
centre. Odd
digits prodding sockets, inner
ear's even keel. Eely
fevers no anal
-gesic can truly cure.
Half-mask of numbness.
Immaculate
javelin spurring nerves. Emergency, air—bare
-knuckled. Plucky Apollo rests on your
laurels, *The Hours* in your lap—medusa-pulse,
medusa-pulse. Migraineur—the drawn-out vowels
nauseate you—Virginia Woolf's
one too. Five times you fail to reach a salty doctor's
pointer finger. One two five days—you're still craving
quietness, quietness. Whiteness
raves and Melbourne
-shuffles, spills its smiley
talcum powder on your stern
-um. You fail to record sensitivity
(vampiric) to sunlight, unfurling in a
whirlpool, *cupio dissolvi*
—xerostomia. The doctor records letters—all Greek to
you. In the gods
Zeus fashions another thunderclap.

Petrarchan Sonnet

In Roma—*Hannibal ad portas! Aie!*
—I flared between dazzled cats, through cobblestoned
streets, Chianti-red dragon, classically stoned,
tripped until dawn, bearing purple tie-dye
pants, shirt, black beret. *Cry
-baby, Mama's Boy!* my untoned
body scolded. Black coffee intoned
Latin prayers in the hotel restaurant. I

didn't want to advance on Russia, see
The Motherland Calls' horror, the Kremlin,
care for the Soviet controllers' reign.
The Cure's 'From The Edge Of The Deep Green Sea'
was devoured by my Walkman's gremlin,
Aeroflot's winged hammer and sickle scoured black rain.

Tritina after The Cure

In the photograph you're mimicking Bogie. It's
the last summer of harmony. The black dog's not
in shot, nor's the red-lipped *fidus Achates* you

met in the '80s. Their allegros are. God, you
smoked handsomely, blue-eyed Sandboy. Though it's
been thirteen months since you made waves, I cannot

widen *We're*. Homer honoured the Nereids but not
Nerites and Poseidon's soulful love. Did you
as you dissolved in gold? Life at the Earth's end—it's

snowless, it's easy, not austere. Wind sings. Do you?

The 52-hertz Whale

My soul is exceeding sorrowful, even unto death
Matthew 26:38

Is it grotesque or aesthetic? Is it lonely,
the oceans' sorrowful soul? What is its gender,
its species? Is it hybrid? Virtuosic? Unique?

•

Thirty-odd years now you've tracked me
as convoys of krill, those vertical ploughers, track currents. It's
    solitude
I crave. I've quelled your accelerometer.
In International Klein Blue I thrash my queer tuba.

Your aquarium would still me, its fearful air you.
There'll be no silly Hallmark
card or plush toy available for purchase from Kmart.

Duplex

Welwitschia mirabilis

My two broad leaves will shoot for centuries,
adoring night's bite, exciting day's blaze.

>Adoring nights bite, exciting days blaze
>—my ample taproot orchestrates sand-songs.

Man wants to sample my taproot's sand-songs,
wonders How can you advantage me, Plant?

>I am wondrous—always *Advantage, Plant*.
>I can withstand Man, thalassic mysteries.

Man, you cannot stand Jurassic mysteries.
Is your one undiminished wish *To be*?

>My one undiminished wish is to be
>unattended, crooning 'The Onion Song'.

Unattended, crooning 'The Onion Song',
my two broad leaves will shoot for centuries.

Sestina: Love

Every poet idolises Like, but Love
is the vivider figure. When Like tries to buy Love
Love yawns, hums 'The Things We Do For Love'.
Like's green-eyed as The Dreadful Flying Glove,
spiky as The Four-Headed Bulldog, Love
the polyglot that grows roseate love.

Like loves to let go, to get high on love
boat, Love likes to gulp whole bowls of love
apples while grappling with **VOTE NO TO FREE LOVE!**
Nightly, Like plays the same game with Love
(Anagrams). Like writes *To hamper*, Love
I smile. Like flies off the handle, snaps *Love*

*is a many-splendored thing! Be a love
and put a little love in your heart*, urges Love,
unballing rainbow socks. Like, toxic as Love
Canal, Niagara Falls, wants to clip their red-faced love
-birds' wings, Love to make love
beads, soya bread loaves and clove

-wort crowns. *Eat your heart out, Love,*
Like laughs, *I'll always be younger!* Love
shrugs, puts on its scarf, its red left glove,
its right, straightens a daguerreotype of Love
-lace, Ada, musses its hair. The yellow foxglove
tolls as arpeggiated Love

strolls down the garden path, untrussing love
-in-a-mist's stars, sowing the seeds of love
-grass. The solitary berry of truelove
whirls. *Yes, Like? I just called to say I love—
Yew?* Love returns home, twirls to 'Digital Love'.
Like rolls its eyes. *You hate that I love*

in any language. Like clucks its tongue, *You love
helter-skelter, sweetheart.* The look of Love
could melt tungsten. *You really do love
the sound of your own voice,* scolds Love,
booking a one-way ticket to Love
-land, Colorado. *You bastard. I unlove

you,* spits slovenly Like. *Stop!* signs Love,
in the name of love. In their beat-up LUV
Like stares east. Golden plovers pair for Love.

A TREE SINGS

Agave americana

A Decaying Sestina after and for Lawrence Schimel

I am not a centenarian.
A decade or two, three at most.
I know my place. I am of the New
World. Do not mix me up with *Aloe
vera*, whose adhesiveness disturbs me.
I have captured the verdigris

and spikes of Lady Liberty. Degree
by revered degree the sun, the one latitudinarian,
cultivates its goldfield. *Cyme!*
it announces. I almost
flounce and stalk upwards. Though alo

-ne and single-minded I am happy as a low
-altitude cloud or the man swirling pinot gris
on his modernist portico. The lowermost
atoms animate me, ultimate utilitarian,

utterly unmoved by apiarian
tongues. Suddenly I spurt skywards. Below,
the man gasps. Grasping the middlemost

CO_2 I surge. Showily I unfold my gold in this, the uppermost,
sphere. My capsules fade to black. Superior libertarian,

my shiny, black seeds blow, every one agrarian.

Hills Hoist

Over moist grass it windmills its arms. The way you clutch one sends chills up my spine. My laughter doesn't go unvoiced. *A no-frills cousin was the only thing left standing in Alawa after Cyclone Tracy.* Across the country, other clotheslines rejoiced! A gust fills an almost-hung out T-shirt, the clouds are revoiced. *Blue pegs for blues! I'll make you do it my way,* you tease, *even if it kills me. His shouts and claps outvoiced the deep-mouthed sea* ... A boisterous wind picks up, colour mills about. *Swinging on Mum's was one of childhood's biggest thrills. I'll bet she voiced her annoyance* ... In the sunroom we pogo to a song about dollar bills. Exposed ceiling joists ripple. After dinner, a black comedy set in Royston Vasey, then the latest Nils Frahm. The bedroom's where we cloister ourselves to meditate—a '60s Mistral fan wills calm. *You're good for me*, I say drowsily, *like the gills of green oysters.* You kiss my mottled eyebrows, Buenas noches, *whippoorwills. Consider yourself invoiced.* I turn over, knowing the sharkish stills won't foist themselves upon me while I sleep. In the small hours a Japanese carrier roisters, spills oil into Mauritian waters.

In the navy

> *(i.m. Stuart Addison, Steven Bebbington,
> Jake Casey, Brett Dwyer, Ewen McDonald)*

shipmates hang me over the stern
—the propeller's a sort of halo
urging *Fight and win at sea!*
every eyeball's bright with ice

The propeller's a sort of halo
I'm ordered to worship, worship
Every eyeball's bright with ice
chemical burns get worse, get worse

Aboard this godawful warship
water and food's withheld
chemical burns become a curse
I learn how not to make waves

Water and food's withheld
the AF leaves me high and dry
I learn how not to make waves
in the navy. In the navy

the AF leaves me high and dry
shipmates hang me over the stern
Hell's the navy, Hell's the navy
urging *Fight and win at sea!*

Moby-Dick; or, The Whale

I
regard
this
as
queer.

Queer
eye,
ass,
regard
this ...

this
queer
regard.
Eye
ass,

ass
—his.
I
queer
regard,

regard
as
queer
this
eye.

I regard his
ass, queer.

I really hope you're doing okay

(A Decaying Sestina after and for Benjamin Dodds)

during these totally bizarre times.
It's like something out
of The Andromeda Strain.
Not like real life at all.
How is life
in your quarantined state?

In this critical state
I've applied sheer stress—the worst time's
atmosphere's deliquesced—life's
elements are CH(N)OPS-smacking & out
-numbering, Mr Smith's gall

-ium-glowing noble hands appall
-ing me; it's whipping me into a *state*,
that liquid word; beakers are spout
-ing black snakes, blazing time's

crazy oscillations; on the TV screen time's
classic symbol's flickering & red, Mr Smith's pall
-adic crown's having a gas, *Rent the VHS—Out,*

Lewis!—Extra mark on the plasma test—Out!
—for the first berk who reports the film's ending. Time's

thallium's pal, he'd warn, spectral, lining the best of times.

#8WordStory

Two men kiss. Confetti. The moon rises, sets.

Cerberus Watches Eros

His flower watering's driving me to the brink.
I'm in three minds. Gore his crude cacophony?
Flaunt these eely implants? Exude my foulest stink?
His flower watering's driving me to the brink.
What the hell. Unseal the door, don't let him drink
wine, plant him in the Mourning Fields, no coffin. He,
his flower watering's driving me to the brink.
Three minds chime in. Gore his crude cacophony!

At Seven Mile Beach

(With a nod to Timothy Conigrave)

I walked between you and the sea, holding
in one hand a piece of driftwood, in the
other a loop of your blue jeans. A man

studied us as if we were subhuman.
God, I idolised your never-holding
-back. Twenty-four years later you packed the

mourners in, but I couldn't control the
bodies' salt and water. Superhuman
holding-off was my noted season, holding

-on, holding-on yours, lithe protean man.

Duplex

> *And if a house be divided against itself,*
> *that house cannot stand.*
>
> Mark 3:25

In the beginning I was a house
of God. Frankincense pieces were swung

> by ikons. Sweet Jesus, can sense be swung
> into the heathens who tenant me now?

Impenitent heathens. Split in two now
I am beside myself, far from detached.

> I am beside myself—I feel detached
> from the carpenter who bore my tongue

and groove, never talked with a forked tongue,
and built the Four Evangelists up.

> I can't handle this tilted discord. Up
> pipes St Mark: *A house divided can't stand.*

I pipe *A house divided can't stand.*
In the beginning I was a house.

Little Gilt

after Charles Marelle and Edgar Allan Poe

Once upon a bleary midnight, a fearless young man with a buzz cut bewitchingly gold as his grandfather's entered The Wood, where flirty older men were frisking about to soulful house. Raoul gently shouldered past these bears and cubs, then parted purple curtains, revealing a cheery cocktail lounge. *Shot of Goldschläger, please.* The lone wolf stood aside and tilted his head. *Boy oh boy, you're a ray of sunshine.* Raoul noted the hairy arms, the big tongue, the oiled mutton chops, remembered the rough voice, the searing *Little Lamb*, the vase of wilted Easter daisies. His foot kept time with the snare drum. *Two more, please. No, no—one for me, one for my friend with the great white teeth.* Not a single bit of alcohol was spilt. *Water!* bleated the wolf, scouring the bar as if he'd gulped yellow coals. Piece of cake, Raoul thought, emerging from the belly of the club. A neon sign—Pallas, a built centaur—speared its glow around him. *'Police, Fire or Ambulance?'* Raoul called his father next. *Nevermore*, he said to the pretty stars, disposing of body parts and nursery rhyme, shards of flowers, glass and guilt. The black Sonata drew nearer. *Nevermore.*

The morning fog

is sweetest at the Tropic of Capricorn,
the colour of lemon chiffon
cake, and just as delicate. It might upspring
with a ringing of hands, it might upspring
with a single step. It's capable of taking
itself to the streets. Unblighted
by African tulip trees' jewels, the palms
look as if they're about to take flight.
Vehicles' steel appeals to the atmosphere.
We, too, are aerial now. We needn't be
momentarily. Where does it end, where
does it upspring, this enlightening
thing unfurling its whorls. Even
to rusty furrows it's in
-clined to breathe. Subtleties
emerge as if soaked in developer, but slower.
Though we look before and after, and pine
for what is not, we alight on the *I*
of Horsfield's Bushlark widening to *We*,
its rites of day- and night-time melody and mimicry,
and I ask you crave nothing
save the song and wing-heeled being
as brightness wheels around the mountain.

Luna, *Taxus baccata*

after Sylvia Plath's 'The Moon and the Yew Tree'

One packs sandwiches in the
Tupperware so airtight it might be moon
-suitable, the other pours milk and
freshly brewed Brazil Santos into the
Thermos. *I hope we see a yew
tree*, says one. *I want to be a tree!*

sings the other. Tree
after tree rings as they stir the
highway. *Graves called the yew
tree the death-tree. And the moon
—car in P—the Goddess of the
Sky.* They cross the road and

buy Cornettos and
lie under a Christmas tree,
one of thirteen overseeing the
beach and bristling with the
twinned rainbow lorikeets quaffing moon
after odd-shaped moon. *Yew*

*leaves're poisonous, yew
bark, yew wood. The arils aren't, and
Shakespeare called the yew double-fatal. A moon
of ice cream sends birds into orbit. The tree
ho ho hos. One sits up. What's that, on the
horizon? Constellation of the*

heart— Enlarging ... The
two men thicken, a yew
hedge. The moon rises like the
sun. (Distracted by drunks and
disorderlies consuming the tree,
they'd forgotten the moon.)

Oh my God, it's the moon—
Red as an aril ... Around it, the
clouds're branches of a tree
—Taxus baccata, *European yew.*
The men watch the moon redden and
spark, the yew tree smoke. Whispers one to the

other, *The moon ... I'm over the*
moon. I think you hung the moon and
the stars. It's an astounding tree, the yew.

Sonnet 29

'Bruce'? Unforgettable, but 'In Your Eyes'
I don't remember, or the New York state
trio, or 'I Don't Remember', or cries
of 'Boum', but I played the one that tells fate
on Sunday afternoon, and Weber's hope
-anthem, and 'Let Me Love You', you self-possessed
while talking about the flexible scope,
dialysis (*A thrill to say the least*),
fearing God again, and Hell, despising
your deeds, but if anyone died in a state
of grace it was you (too young to hear sing,
with a great deal of feeling, at the Village Gate,
Blossom Dearie, whose whisper brings
on morning wings), O king of kings.

Duplex

    Emperor penguin (*Aptenodytes forsteri*)

Bone-whiteness flowered among the ice
overconfident. Eggs, pouched, pear-shaped,

    were poached on our continent, pear-shaped,
    more chicks killed by the Giant Petrol

Spill than the southern giant petrel,
more by the orange South Polar Skewer

    than the orange-mawed south polar skua,
    more adults by flip-top bottles' seals

than hulking, hotly-flippered leopard seals.
Shapeshifters evaporated floes.

    Shapeshifters ate evaporites' flows
    -heets. Formless chorus, we sing the blue's

heat. Formless chorus, we sing the blues.
Bone-whiteness flowers among the ice.

Old Habits Die Hard

Every weekday afternoon, while my father swam laps, my mother and I would laze in recliners and scoop homemade French onion dip with Jatz Crackers. The way she'd move the nail file from digit to digit without tilting her gaze from *The Young and the Restless* was mesmerising—so too the hopeful glint of its grooved stainless steel. Did Mrs Cashion hide it in a fruit cake? I'd sometimes wonder. My brother the crazy quilter still picks his fingernails until blood floods the lunulae—his nail beds are cratered as the moon. I've been biting mine since middle school. Not even the solution my mother would apply to the unholy mess could stop me. I grew to enjoy its bitterness as I grew to enjoy grapefruit's. Psychiatrists insist trichotillomania goes hand in hand with onychophagia, but recently I met my eyebrowless ex who otherwise resembles Johnny Marr and who's only ever clipped his fingernails. *I tweeze them*, he said. *The Zoloft's useless*. I started plucking my left one after the accident. *You look like Aquaman*, Kane said, prodding my bald patch as we exited the cinema. The course of true love never did run smooth. Thank God I'm able.

From the Morning

Breathing in this cattle town
agrees with me. Onto my street
gush bottlebrushes, rightfully blood
-bright. 'Blood Roses'
discloses *You have what*

it takes, small ball for
twenty years. Napoleon
B's got your back.
Things cluster like cutlery,
jet-black, stingless, powdery. *Shh!*

they say to the five men with
skulls featureless as ivory
billiard balls, blood moon-throats
and side-lancing bootsoles.
Scarlet hibiscus-trumpets call off

the hounds. The clouds
mull over their armament—deserts
of lapwings, water-platter tree
-s' melting peltate leaves, Pom
-eranians' miniature thunder.

•

In the beginning the lion of God,
clothed as a sheepdog,
rose up against me. Dopey pack-dog,
I couldn't resist. Fists, back. Worn ivory
shock absorbers cowered from every body.

The Panzerschokolade high,
the wurst of Germany
adored me, but I was secondary magenta,
felt like a penny
waiting for change, crossed

a Rubicon with an eight ball.
My careless stems cultivated prickles,
my honeycomb
was moulded by killer stings' speedballs. A station
trained in the arcs

of the heart declared my country
independent. I salted a universal fall
of needlepoint ivy,
withdrew my inculpable army,
adopted the Code Napoleon.

•

Another midwinter victory.
The crimson bougainvillea hangs up its hat
on the apostrophes of the sea,
an irrepressible generals
-hip. Niches

of cerumen dis
-tinguish soft bodies,
the flawless upholstery
shines. *This is no mausoleum.*
This is a coffin in Egypt, opine

the engineers. The thousand smiles
of *Grevillea* 'Moonlight' are practical
as bodyguards mummifying small
intruders. Brimming receptacles
are attended by me

-liponines, fine bobby pins.
These bees taste my honour
-ability. The hive speaks its mind
And now we rise and we are. Everything
I taste is trusting and Titian as honey.

Happiness

    for Felicity Plunkett

transformation happening as if marble turns to flesh
everything you give off moving faster than purest desert light
taking on a bluer tinge, a sculpted shape
and you infolding the world like it's a shape more familiar than air
opening up exactly what's required
making a mountain out of gravity's falling tissue
reorganising   how the heat takes over
gliding over stone and the shadows of those passing
the hillsides like a breath
drumming its fists on the verandah roof
and certainly patching up those palm-tree tops with far-off cumulus

    •

carrying the thought of you, the touch of you,
body held explored crotch and cock
how you look at me   how you look back

    •

outside the window
honey-eaters, blue wrens,
bouquets of white cockatoos bursting from the leaves
their speed so fine they look like dark flames

    •

A drover playing his harmonica
to the flesh's range,
immense like Australian sky

    •

words turning out later to be the simplest thoughts:
when I was born
like a ghost or a short, quick river
into country without water apart from winter rain
shaping and reshaping sideways through winter sun's white light –
recalled just now
a neighbour – what are they doing out there? – dropping a trailer or a drum

•

knowing the world's renewable despite each paid-off politician.
on a backdrop of night,
they know nothing of life's burning colour.

•

suddenness which takes my breath away
(the slow dissolve, daybreak light on clouds like broccoli leaves)
the poem for you
meeting the air
The last view of the sea

•

We farmed it like we were angels.

You're

a cardinal wing tilting sideways for
a sodden-spined god on an airy desk.
That fathomless ichthyocentaur.

A volatile, icy body pour
-ing its hair up into picturesque
churn. An unfeeling Antarctic core.

Foam cartwheeling the rafts of the Coeur
d'Alene. A pilgrim bottle, grotesque
-embellished. The mortar and pestle of moonlore.

The portable barre, the Adagio floor,
the most fluid arabesque.
Snow crunching beyond the big war

-drobe. Whetstone of fastest wild boar.
County Waterford's Romanesque.
Pearl the albino raven's caw.

My lucky charm, an anointed rabbit paw.
Apollo, miniature, Pythian, statuesque.
The white of my eye, my dropping jaw.
Only a whale, not a metaphor.

A Night Like This

Like God, I'm over it
—the moon, that is. To say
I'm cheerful as a rainbow
is an understatement

The moon (that is to say
the queerest mirror ball)
has been understated
don't you think, on a night like this?

The queerest mirror ball
overlooks me, one hundred-eyed Argos
Don't you think, on a night like this
I'm overworked and overdressed?

I'm overlooked, one hundred-eyed Argos
I'm over 40, over 65 kilos too
I'm overworked and overdressed
—send in stitchers

I'm over 40, over 65 kilos too
I'm cheerful as a rainbow
-'s end, in stitches,
like God. I'm over it

Daphne's Tritina

Did I shake like a leaf? Was I rooted to the
spot? My limbs passed arrows, trimmed a steel cage
for the suicidal son who Lady

Tina bowed. She branched and branched his malady
for fun. Four weeks of gnash and thrash, of seethe and *Breathe,
darlin', breathe.* One Sunday, in a boscage,

a stranger stopped me. *How could you encage
your baby! Walk a mile in my heels, lady.*
My boy and I don't rest on our laurels, wreathe

regrets. No epithet's a cage for this lady.

Pentina after The Beatles

for Matt Hetherington

All
you
need
is
love.

Love,
all
is
U
-kneed.

Knead
love
—yew,
awl,
Is

-is
—knead
all.
Love
you!

You!
Is
love
need
-all?

All you need
is love.

Moon's Étude

Pink balloon? Clewed wool?
Unsmooth supper plate?

Sinker of cliché
in cumulous seas.

I loose jewelleries,
unlike Saturn, a

gold-fattened linger
-er. *Monsieur Aloof!*

Again, you finger
-point. *Murderer!* Oof.

*When you're full, you're full
of yourself!* you blaze.

I routinely skate
closer to the prot

-ostars. I am not
going through a phase.

Immortal Jellyfish

> *I ask'd thee, 'Give me immortality.'*
> Alfred, Lord Tennyson, 'Tithonus'

Pinkie fingernail-small. No brain, all brawn.
I bloom in ballast water, bell awake
in a cell a far cry from the marquee
of the sea. You goggle at, prod my art
—unfussed, cruciate, scarlet. *Have a heart,*
you pray, aspiring Tithonuses. *Make
known to us your mystery.* Let me be
crystal clear—just the unfeared can redawn.

Duplex

> *Nothing of him that doth fade,*
> *But doth suffer a sea-change*
> *Into something rich and strange.*
>
> Shakespeare, *The Tempest*

My rapist's name was Hebrew—Lion of God.
He told me I laughed like his missing uncles.

    I miss the rolling laughter of uncles
    who acted marvellously in *The Tempest*.

Cyclone Marcia, too, was a five-act tempest.
I charted the shaking, the aerial earth.

    In Shakespeare's Ariel's chart there's no earth.
    My rapist was born under Capricorn.

I wonder at the Tropic of Capricorn.
I sea-swim, I see the sea change in spring.

    I sea-swim, I see the sea change in spring.
    I ring an interstate detective.

I state to an interviewing detective
My rapist's name was Hebrew—Lion of God.

Boys Don't Cry

```
                                        O
                                        nce upon
                                        a time, a boy leapt into
                                        a poster's figure,
                                        a poster's figure a boy
                                    F   lamboyancy! The boy
                                        was teased for teasing
                                        his hair: Nancy boy!
                                        For his 16th   birth
                                          day the boy    re
                                        ceived a guitar from
                                        his wandering father A
                                        Bm C♯m D Doesn't mean
                                        you're one of the boys spat
            a mean boy                  C♯m Bm C♯m Bm C♯m Bm
            The boy                     practised morning noon night
                      His tea           cher pinched his calluses: Be
                           a man!       Callousness appalled the boy
                                so gay-boyishly enthralled by a pall
                                bearer's leggiero step he didn't
                                pick his guitar for two weeks
                                Too weak to fight back? The boy
                                scout sprouted horns The strung
                                out   guitar enraptured the beast
                                    E    F♯m E F♯m F♯m7 F♯m
                                    The boy boiled The guitar
                                    zipped its black jacket,
                                    buoyed up E F♯m D E
                                    At twenty,  high on E
                                    and grief,   the boy
                                    snapped     off the
                                    neck of    his guitar
                                    Oh boy!    said the
                                    boy's boy   friend
                                    Boys will    be boys
                                    The boy    distilled
                                    grief: a pa   per sheaf
                                    That's my   boy! said
                                    the boy's    still father
                                    Now,       the boy
                                    joyfully    wanders
                                    around    with his head
                                    in the clouds  In the clouds
                                    are wonders A Bm C♯m D
                                    C♯m Bm A
```

Coffee Grounds

The percolator burns my hands.
Should I exfoliate my skin,
or scour our blue Le Creuset pans?

Console the mushrooms (*Folding fans!*)
whose caps are bowed and colours thin?
The percolator burns my hands.

Perhaps I'll buff the hardwood trans
-verse, reinforce the earthworms' inn.
A scattering around the pans

-ies, more upon the hearth's afghans?
The record spirals violin,
the percolator burns my hands,

a memory ex-ex-expands
(the affogato of Turin
that my rare green bean, and Japan's,

undrowned with flair; my *Ciaos!* to flans),
con-con-contracts. The coffee in
the percolator burns. My hands
reheat his sweet biscotti pans.

Transcontinental Truth Ghazal

The globe pins to its peaked lapels truth
-ovals, spins itself, then stairwells truth.

Saké, shoyu and steam seduce a
Japanese littleneck clam shell's truth.

Like trumpeters, twin-domed elephants
buzz, but the tusker alone smells truth.

Onto the Serengeti blood spills
the hyaena and the gazelle's truth.

The ochre bells of the jellyfish
tree dehisce and hiss the Seychelles' truth.

Only banana leaf wallpaper
grasps The Beverly Hills Hotel's truth.

Illusion belts out 'Who's Afraid Of
Virginia Woolf?', then well-wells Truth.

The hair of a southern Chilean
succulent flares its lemon bells' truth.

Its capacity to rock may be
a Galápagos tortoise shell's truth.

Antarctic drifters and wanderers
bloom, clean forgetting single cells' truth.

White, swivelling nibs—a colossal,
tubular, undersea inkwell's truth.

Gloucestershire's daffodil showboats, but
the poet's daffodil retells truth.

Silver nets in fresh water, diving
bell spiders secrete hydrogels' truth.

A superb lyrebird reinterprets
Jagger's flashes and parallels truth.

Yellow crazy ants or toxicants?
(The Christmas Island pipistrelle's truth.)

The globe neatens its bright tuxedo,
stands on the landing, then kvells. *Truth.*

Notes on Form

Like to the Lark's working title was 'Form & Function', after Photek's drum & bass record of the same name. Music and sound, form and transformation underpin the collection; its cornerstone is the sonnet ('from Italian *sonetto*, "little song," from Latin *sonus* "sound"'). 'Form', writes Felicity Plunkett, 'is concerned with de- and re-arranging, working between what has gone and what is to come. It is about connection and generation.' Form is Gwen Harwood's 'trellis' and 'fine pumpkins'. It is stave and symphony, wooden last and Ferragamo Rainbow Sandal, scaffold and Golden Gate Bridge. Every form flaunts its uniform, kaleidoscopic or otherwise.

The phrase 'like to the lark' is from Shakespeare's 'Sonnet 29', a poem important to Sandy Mitchell, one of my book's dedicatees, and to me. My 'Sonnet 29', an elegy for Sandy, is also a terminal, a form invented by John Tranter. 'Terminals borrow the end-words of each line of their source poems,' explains David McCooey. 'By employing fragments of pre-existing texts to generate new texts, [they are] by definition endlessly shape-shifting, and therefore paradoxically "formless".'

My poem 'The Pardoner' is a terminal from Sylvia Plath's 'The Jailer'. Two lines from the latter—'I have been drugged and raped. / Seven hours knocked out of my right mind'—echo crimes I experienced in the mid-1990s. This date-rape and the later gang-rape I survived are illuminated in other poems, e.g., 'Sestina: Rape'. The traditional sestina has six end-words but 'Sestina: Rape' has only one—'rape' (or a true rhyme of, e.g., 'crêpe', 'scrape', 'drape'). My intention in writing the poem was to desensitise myself to the word that tormented me for decades, without diminishing its power.

The Lawrence Schimel-designed Decaying Sestina sheds a line a stanza and was the ideal form for my Decaying Sestina '*Agave americana*', in which the plant witnesses its own flourishing and fading. Conceived by Marie Ponsot and Rosemary Deen, the tritina comprises three tercets and a one-line envoi. The form is urgent—in 'Daphne's Tritina' my feminist revision of the myth of Daphne and Apollo collides with my account of a Rockhampton woman's love of her meth-addicted son. The titles of some of my favourite songs, books and poems are woven as end-words into other tritinas (e.g., The Cure's 'It's Not You' into 'Tritina after The Cure', Timothy Conigrave's *Holding the Man* into 'At Seven Mile Beach') and sestinas (e.g., Sylvia Plath's 'The Moon and the Yew Tree' into 'Luna, *Taxus baccata*', Belinda Carlisle's 'Heaven Is A Place On Earth' into 'Sestina after B. Carlisle').

In the pantoum, lines echo spell-like between stanzas, simultaneously contracting and expanding the form's energies ('Persian Love Cake', 'Moon Speaks during Pasur'), and subtle changes to one line's spelling and punctuation can radically reshape meaning ('In the navy', 'A Night Like This'). Similarly, the incantatory rhymes and refrain of the rondelet ('diminutive of *rondel*, "short poem with a refrain," literally "small circle"') narrow and widen the form's focuses ('Central Queensland Rondelets').

Duplex architect Jericho Brown describes his creation as 'a ghazal that is also a sonnet that is also a blues poem'—three forms I adore. 'Resilience in the face of hardship is one of the hallmarks of the blues poem' (poets.org)—and, accordingly, the duplex. Of *Like to the Lark*'s eight duplexes, four are about tenacious plants from their own points of view, one an acquaintance living with HIV, one a duplex that used to be a church, one about otherworldly emperor penguins and one my reporting my first rape to a detective.

Writing these duplexes encouraged me to make two new forms. My poems 'Sketching Aids'—which blends three memories of an ex-boyfriend—and 'Dinner with S. M. at Tandoori Den'—which depicts our final meal together three years before his death—are terse-sets. The first four and a half lines of the former poem sprung up while I was looking at old photographs. The arrangement of 'queen' and 'between' suggested the ABC rhyme scheme and tercets. An eruption of grief insisted on the need for concision in the form of trisyllabic lines. The terse-set—my pun on tercet—is made up of a minimum of three tercets. Its form is playful but its content sober. Its language is precise, clear and simple, like the Imagists'.

'Killing Bill or Whatever the Hell His Name Is ("Battle Without Honor or Humanity")', which describes the cruelty encountered by an acquaintance following his disclosing his HIV+ status to a lover, is a flashbang—a synonym of an explosive named in the poem. The flashbang is composed of a minimum of four unrhymed, uneven couplets bisected by a bullet (•). The first set of couplets presents a crisis, the second a solution, if there is one. Every couplet's first line—the flash—consists of two or more words, every second line—the bang—of only one. The flash mirrors a thrown explosive's arc, the bang its detonation. The flashbang's form is disorientating but its content unambiguous. Its language corresponds to the terse-set's.

The terse-set and the flashbang concern adversity but are at heart declarations of resilience. Making them was crucial not only to the development of my writing but also to the deepening of my ability to sit with grief and to articulate anger. I needed new language—new forms—in order to try to comprehend this loss of life, this prejudice. Meditating on elegy, responsibility and respect was key.

For me, writing in form, 'flexing the form'—a phrase from Sandra Beasley's essay on the sestina—and creating forms are fascinating, exhilarating and liberating. Forms are 'instruments of discovery,' said Marie Ponsot, who was fond of writing in tritinas, sestinas and villanelles. '[They] create an almost bodily pleasure in the poet. They are not restrictive. They pull things out of you.' Forms are microscope and telescope, stethoscope and seismometer, *Fantastic Voyage*'s *Proteus* and NASA's Voyager 1.

Bon voyage!

References

Sandra Beasley, 'Flexing the Form: Contemporary Innovation in the Sestina', poets.org, October 1, 2018.

'Blues Poem', Glossary, poets.org.

Jericho Brown, 'Invention', poetryfoundation.org, March 18, 2019.

Gwen Harwood, 'At Mornington', *Collected Poems 1943–1995*, St Lucia: UQP, 2013.

David McCooey, 'Review Short: John Tranter's *Heart Starter*', *Cordite Poetry Review*, August 25, 2015.

Felicity Plunkett, 'True to Form: A. E. Stallings, Jenny Xie, Ada Limón', *Sydney Review of Books*, October 30, 2019.

'Roundelay', Online Etymology Dictionary.

Dinitia Smith, 'Recognition at Last for a Poet of Elegant Complexity', *The New York Times*, April 13, 1999.

'Sonnet', Online Etymology Dictionary.

Notes

The dedication's first epigraph is from E. E. Cummings' '[as is the sea marvelous]', *Tulips and Chimneys* (Thomas Seltzer, 1923), the second from Ruggero Leoncavallo's *Pagliacci*, both in the public domain.

The first epigraph is from David Malouf's 'Revolving Days' from *Typewriter Music* (St Lucia: UQP, 2007), used with the kind permission of UQP, the second from Virginia Woolf's *Mrs Dalloway* (Hogarth Press, 1925), which is in the public domain.

'Off-world Ghazal': the epigraph 'I could hear / the wild black cockatoos, tossed on the crest / of their high trees, crying the world's unrest.' is from Judith Wright's 'Black Cockatoos', *Collected Poems* (HarperCollins Publishers, 2016), used with the kind permission of HarperCollins Publishers Australia Pty Limited. The poem contains fragments of Kahlil Gibran's *The Prophet* (Alfred A. Knopf, 1923): 'giant oak', 'sealed [...] records', 'nights when earth was up-wrought.' 'Stars thrown from an arc interrupt—' reworks 'stars thrown dark / And lifeless from an interrupted arc.' from Robert Frost's 'A Star in a Stone-boat'. *The Prophet* and 'A Star in a Stone-boat' are in the public domain.

'Abecedarian on Tension': the epigraph 'the wrecked thing that could / not bear the light nor hide / hobbled in its own blood.' is from Gwen Harwood's 'Barn Owl', *Collected Poems 1943–1995* (St Lucia: UQP, 2013), used with the kind permission of John Harwood.

'Double Acrostic': the epigraph 'Did he who made the Lamb make thee?' is from William Blake's 'The Tyger', which is in the public domain. '¡Ándale! ¡Arriba!' is part of the cry of Speedy Gonzales, a Warner Bros. *Looney Tunes* and *Merrie Melodies* cartoon character.

'Curtal Sonnet' remixes some of the text from ENTRIP Consumer Medicines Information http://www.mydr.com.au/medicines/cmis/entrip-tablets.

'The Pardoner' is a terminal from, and contains the end-words of, Sylvia Plath's 'The Jailer'. 'My own mind is my own church' is from Thomas Paine's *The Age of Reason; Being an Investigation of True and Fabulous Theology*, 'a kelson of the creation' from Walt Whitman's 'Song of Myself', 'such sweet thunder' from Shakespeare's *A Midsummer Night's Dream*, all in the public domain.

'A–Z–A': 'arsenic (n.), late 14c., "yellow arsenic, arsenic trisulphide," from Old French *arsenic*, from late Greek *arsenikon* "arsenic", from Old Iranian **zarna-* "golden,"' is from Online Etymology Dictionary's entry for 'arsenic'.

'Binary Tree Poem': 'fascinating artificial flavor' and 'now longer-lasting' are two of Wrigley's Juicy Fruit slogans.

'In Heaven I'll be quite normal (or, Pentina to Doone Kennedy, after The Smiths)' was inspired by a December 5, 1988 *Hinch at Seven* interview. In response to the question 'Do you find the idea of men having sex with men or women having sex with women quite offensive?', Doone Kennedy, 67th Lord Mayor of Hobart, said 'I do. I'm quite normal, thank goodness.' The poem refers to 'Why Noel Shot Himself and Bert Went to Gaol', *The Examiner*, March 13, 1976.

'Killing Bill or Whatever the Hell His Name Is (Battle Without Honor or Humanity)': Tomoyasu Hotei's 'Battle Without Honor or Humanity' was included on *Kill Bill Vol. 1 Original Soundtrack* (Warner Bros., 2003). 'A gaze blank and pitiless as the sun' is from W. B. Yeats' 'The Second Coming', which is in the public domain.

'Sestina after B. Carlisle': 'no rest day nor night' is from Revelation 14:11, 'consuming fire' from Hebrews 12:29, 'from Greek *syndromos* place where several roads meet' from Online Etymology Dictionary's entry for 'syndrome'. 'Fuck you very much' was Divine's signature line.

'The Being': the epigraph 'Representatives of the gay community are no better than Saddam Hussein' is from *The Examiner*, February, 1991. 'I am fallen, your arch-villain (but I ought to be your Adam!)' reworks 'I ought to be thy Adam; but I am rather the fallen angel' from Mary Shelley's *Frankenstein; or, The Modern Prometheus*, which is in the public domain.

'Royal Poinciana (*Delonix regia*)': 'limbs sang to them of love' reworks 'branches speak to me of love' from Nat Simon and Buddy Bernier's 'Poinciana (Song of the Tree)', an adaptation of Manuel Lliso's 'La Canción del Árbol'. The poem nods to Sylvia Plath's 'Daddy' and 'Elm'.

'Sestina: Rape': 'Her nape caught in his bill' is from W. B. Yeats' 'Leda and the Swan', which is in the public domain.

'Bop: Apollo and Hyacinthos': 'A bop a day keeps the doctor away' is from Cyndi Lauper's *Cyndi Lauper In Paris* (PolyGram Music Video, 1988).

'Rockhampton': 'the description of Rockhampton as "the city of sin, sweat, and sorrow" is usually attributed to Anthony Trollope, who visited Rockhampton in August 1871. "The valley of sin, sweat, and sorrow" appeared in *Rockhampton Bulletin* in April 1871. Shortly after Trollope's visit, *Rockhampton Bulletin* referred to Rockhampton as "the city of sin, sweat, and sorrow" without mentioning Trollope"' (National Library of Australia, Bib ID 6095211).

'Duplex' ('HIV Used to Be ...') borrows its first line from Alice Park's 'HIV Used to Be a Death Sentence. Here's What's Changed in 35 Years', *TIME*, December 1, 2016.

'Spenserian Sonnet' remixes some of the text from SUMATRAN Consumer Medicines Information https://www.mydr.com.au/medicines/sumatran-tablets.

'Hamlet Without the Prince': 'I am but mad north-north-west. When the wind is southerly I know a hawk from a handsaw' is from Shakespeare's *Hamlet*, which is in the public domain.

'Sestina: Pain': 'I will come by you into Spain' is from Romans 15:28, 'pain flows through to your brush-tip / and there is changed' from Gwen Harwood's 'Seven Philosophical Poems' from *Collected Poems 1943–1995* (St Lucia: UQP, 2013), used with the kind permission of John Harwood.

'The Burnt-out Bougainvillea' is a terminal from, and contains the end-words of, Sylvia Plath's 'The Burnt-out Spa'.

'Duplex' (My two broad leaves ...): in the Herero language *Welwitschia mirabilis* is called *onyanga*, meaning desert onion.

'Hills Hoist': 'His shouts and claps outvoiced the deep-mouthed sea' reworks 'Whose shouts and claps outvoice the deep-mouthed sea' from Shakespeare's *Henry V*, which is in the public domain.

'In the navy' borrows its title from the Village People song of the same name and is dedicated to the memories of five men who took their lives while serving in the Royal Australian Navy.

'*Moby-Dick; or, The Whale*': 'I regard this as queer' is from Herman Melville's *Moby-Dick; or, The Whale*, which is in the public domain.

'The morning fog' borrows its title from the Kate Bush song of the same name. 'We look before and after, and pine for what is not' is from Percy Bysshe Shelley's 'To a Skylark', 'you crave nothing save the song' from George Meredith's 'The Lark Ascending', both in the public domain.

'Luna, *Taxus baccata*': 'death-tree' and 'Goddess of the Sky' are from Robert Graves' *The White Goddess* (Carcanet Press, 1997), used with the kind permission of Carcanet Press, 'double-fatal' from Shakespeare's *Richard II*, which is in the public domain.

'Sonnet 29' is a terminal from, and contains the end-words of, Shakespeare's 'Sonnet 29', which is in the public domain. My 'Sonnet 29' contains two phrases (italicised here) from Aaron Sternfield's 'Village Gate Swings With Triple Decker', *Billboard*, November 26, 1966: 'Her voice was slightly louder than a *whisper*. But she didn't need to shout to hold the audience. Miss Dearie managed to inject *a great deal of feeling* into a limited range.'

'Old Habits Die Hard': 'The course of true love never did run smooth' is from Shakespeare's *A Midsummer Night's Dream*, which is in the public domain.

'From the Morning' is a terminal from, and contains the end-words of, Sylvia Plath's 'The Swarm'. 'And now we rise and we are' is from Nick Drake's 'From The Morning', used with the kind permission of Bryter Music.

'Happiness' is a cento from Martin Harrison's *Happiness*, with one line (in order) from each poem: 'Watching How A Rain Front Stops', 'Paris Poems (3. Leaving Paris)', 'Summer Rain Front, North Coast', 'Paris Poems (1. You Do All These Things For Me)', 'Paris Poems (2. A Park)', 'Orchard Bonfire', 'April', 'Hundreds of K's Of It', 'Paris Poems (5. Cardiogram (May))', 'Dry Grass', 'Aubade', 'Paris Poems (6. Rue Cuvier)', 'In the air's touch, round...', 'A Glance (2. Poplars)', 'Patio', 'Daybreak', 'Wallabies', 'About Bats', 'Climates (2. Traditional)', 'Paris Poems (7. Winter Trees)', 'Two For You (1. "As if I could get..."), 'Thoughts spoken out loud...', 'Paris Poems (4. Waters)', 'Blue Wren Poem', 'By the River', 'Cloud', 'Two-Part Variations', 'White-Tailed Deer', 'Climates (3. Question from the Floor)', 'Afterwords *from Luis Cernuda* (2. Let's Never Try to Love)', 'Afterwords *from Luis Cernuda* (1. White Shadows)', 'White Flowers', 'Poem', 'Milk and Honey', 'A Glance (1. Evening At Home)', 'Two For You (2. A Music)', 'Climates (1. The Price of Wind)'. Used with the kind permission of UWA Publishing.

'You're' responds to a gift—a small whale-shaped white light—from Benjamin 'BMD' Dodds and his partner Carlo.

'Daphne's Tritina': for four weeks in 2015 Rockhampton woman Daphne Finnegan kept her consenting son Wylie, then seventeen and addicted to meth, in a custom-built cage. In her article 'We Are Ticking Time Bombs: Inside Australia's Meth Crisis,' *TIME*, May 3, 2017, Sharon Verghis described Daphne as 'the cage lady'.

'Immortal Jellyfish': the epigraph 'I ask'd thee, "Give me immortality."' is from Alfred, Lord Tennyson's 'Tithonus', which is in the public domain.

'Duplex' (My rapist's name …): the epigraph 'Nothing of him that doth fade, / But doth suffer a sea-change / Into something rich and strange.' is from Shakespeare's *The Tempest*, which is in the public domain.

'Boys Don't Cry' borrows its title and several guitar chord progressions from The Cure song of the same name.

Acknowledgements

This book was written on Darumbal country. I acknowledge the traditional custodians, the Darumbal people, and pay my respects to Elders past and present.

Thank you to the editors of the following publications in which these poems first appeared, some in earlier versions: *Admissions: Voices within Mental Health* (eds David Stavanger, Radhiah Chowdhury, Mohammad Awad), *Alcatraz: An International Anthology of Prose/Poetry* (eds Cassandra Atherton, Paul Hetherington), *The Anthology of Australian Prose Poetry* (eds Cassandra Atherton, Paul Hetherington), *Antipodes* (USA), *Australian Poetry Journal*, *Australian Poetry Anthology Volume 6* (eds Jill Jones, Bella Li), *Volume 7* (eds Yvette Holt, Magan Magan), *Volume 8* (eds Melinda Smith, Sara Saleh), *Volume 9* (eds Lucy Dougan, Michelle Cahill), *Best of Australian Poems 2022* (eds Jeanine Leane, Judith Beveridge), *The Canberra Times*, *Cordite Poetry Review*, *foam:e*, *Going Postal: More than 'Yes' or 'No'* (eds Quinn Eades, Son Vivienne), *Griffith Review*, *Impossible Archetype* (Ireland), *Island Magazine*, *The Language in My Tongue: An Anthology of Australian and New Zealand Poetry* (eds Cassandra Atherton, Paul Hetherington), *Lovejets: Queer Male Poets on 200 Years of Walt Whitman* (ed. Raymond Luczak), *Mascara Literary Review*, *Mollyhouse* (USA), *The Montreal Poetry Prize Anthology 2020* (Canada), *The Moth Magazine* (Ireland), *The Night Heron Barks* (USA), *Numéro Cinq* (Canada), *One Hand Clapping* (UK), *Overland Journal*, *Peril Magazine*, *Pink Cover Zine*, *Plumwood Mountain*, *POETRY* (Chicago), *Poetry Wales*, *Pulped Fiction: An Anthology of Microlit* (ed. Cassandra Atherton), *Rabbit: a journal for nonfiction poetry*, *Resilience: 2021 ACU Prize for Poetry Anthology*, *Scars: An Anthology of Microlit* (ed. Cassandra Atherton), *Southerly Journal*, *Stilts Journal*, *StylusLit*, *The Suburban Review*, *Transnational Literature*, *unfurl*, *Verity La*, *Verity La Anthology No. 2: Embody* (eds Michele Seminara, Robbie Coburn, Laura McPhee-Browne), *The Weekend Australian Review*, *Westerly Magazine* and *Writ Poetry Review*.

Thank you to Mindy Gill, Andy Jackson and Jennifer Harrison, Cassandra Atherton and Paul Hetherington, Toby Fitch, and Emma Rose Smith and Tamryn Bennett for commissioning 'Abecedarian on Provincial Drinking' for *Peril Magazine*, 'From the Morning' for *APJ* 9.2 *'DIS—'*, 'Hills Hoist' for *Alcatraz*, 'Sex & Drugs & Goth Rock & Synth-pop & Hip-hop & New Wave & Funk/Soul Ghazal' for *APJ* 8.2 *'spoken'*, and 'You're' for Red Room Company.

'Cerberus Watches Eros' (as 'Triolet: Cerberus and Eros') was nominated for the 2020 Pushcart Prize. 'GRINDR' was performed at Little Fictions' I Heart LGBTQI, February 14, 2017. '#8WordStory': 'Happiness is black cockatoos squabbling in the eucalypts.' and 'Two men kiss. Confetti. The moon rises, sets.', as selected by Nick Earls, appeared on goa, Brisbane's broadcast roadside digital billboard network, on October 23, 2017 and November 17, 2017, as part of a Queensland Writers Centre campaign. 'Little Gilt' was a finalist in the 2021 NWF/joanne burns Microlit Award. 'Off-world Ghazal' was shortlisted for the 2020 Montreal International Poetry Prize. 'Old Habits Die Hard' was a finalist in the 2019 NWF/joanne burns Microlit Award. 'Sestina after B. Carlisle' was awarded the 2021/22 Gwen Harwood Poetry Prize. 'Sestina: Pain' was shortlisted for the 2021 Australian Catholic University Prize for Poetry. A discussion of 'Sestina: Rape' appeared in Stephen Guy-Bray's *Line Endings in Renaissance Poetry* (Anthem Press, 2022)—special thanks to Stephen.

Thank you to my publisher, Terri-ann White, for her energy, flair and guidance, and for creating, in Upswell Publishing, a glowing home for writers and writing. Thank you to my editor, Felicity Plunkett, for her brilliance, care and generosity, and for thrilling on- and off-page larks. Thank you to Chil3's Becky Chilcott and Betty Joy Richards for their fabulous cover design. For their insight, kindness and encouragement, thank you to Cassandra Atherton, Leigh Backhouse, Vallis Backhouse, Gary Barnes, Marie Barnes, Lisa Brockwell, Carlo Caponecchia, Benjamin 'BMD' Dodds, Nigel Featherstone, Paul Gatt, Heidi Germann, Stephen Guy-Bray, Matt Hetherington, Zachary Humphrey, Rose Hunter, Andy Jackson, Anna Jacobson, Anthony Jarvis, A. Frances Johnson, Jeffrey Kelly, Anthony Lynch, Relle McFarlane, Liz McQuilkin, Chris Mole, Amanda O'Callaghan, Nathanael O'Reilly, Mel Penglase, Debbie Reynolds, Fiona Robertson, Michele Sammut, Michael Scott, David Stavanger, Shane Strange, Therese 'T' Stuart, Katie Watmough, Bree Weizenegger and Jessica L. Wilkinson. Special thanks to Ben, Felicity, Leigh, Matt and Nigel for reading and commenting on earlier versions of the manuscript, which transformed accordingly; to Ali Alizadeh, Natalie Harkin, A. Frances Johnson, Kate Lilley, Anthony Lynch and Maria Takolander for responding so warmly—and so swiftly—to it; and to my mother for proofreading it. Thank you to the writers and editors I've worked with and learned from, especially

Quinn Eades, Claire Gaskin, Charmaine Papertalk Green, Jacinta Le Plastrier, Kent MacCarter, Jessica L. Wilkinson and Daniel Young. To my poetry communities, to all at Queensland Poetry and Queensland Poetry Festival, thank you.

About Upswell

Upswell Publishing was established in 2021 by Terri-ann White as a not-for-profit press. A perceived gap in the market for distinctive literary works in fiction, poetry and narrative non-fiction was the motivation. In her years as a bookseller, writer and then publisher, Terri-ann has maintained a watch on literary books and the way they insinuate themselves into a cultural space and are then located within our literary and cultural inheritance. She is interested in making books to last: books with the potential to still be noticed, and noted, after decades and thus be ripe to influence new literary histories.

About this typeface

Book designer Becky Chilcott chose Foundry Origin not only as a strong, carefully considered, and dependable typeface, but also to honour her late friend and mentor, type designer Freda Sack, who oversaw the project. Designed by Freda's long-standing colleague, Stuart de Rozario, much like Upswell Publishing, Foundry Origin was created out of the desire to say something new.

www.ingramcontent.com/pod-product-compliance
Lightning Source LLC
Chambersburg PA
CBHW030842090426
42737CB00009B/1071